Sports Illustrated KIDS

THE ULTIMATE GUIDE TO PRO HOCKEY TEAMS

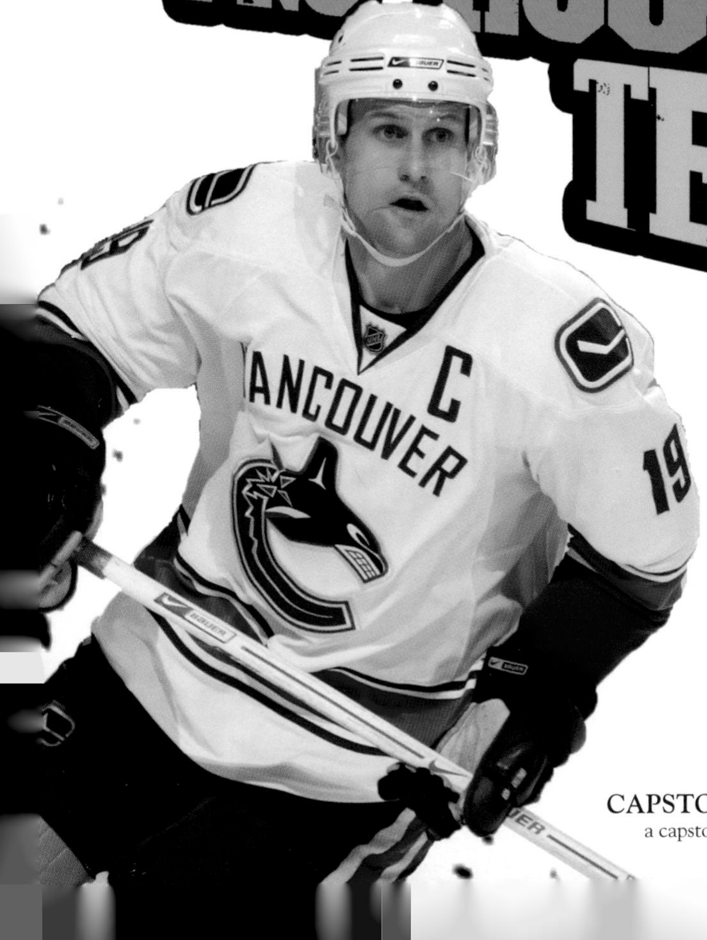

by Shane Frederick

CAPSTONE PRESS
a capstone imprint

Sports Illustrated KIDS Ultimate Pro Team Guides are published
by Capstone Press, 151 Good Counsel Drive, P.O. Box 669,
Mankato, Minnesota 56002. *www.capstonepub.com*

032010
005740CGF10

 Books published by Capstone Press are manufactured with
paper containing at least 10 percent post-consumer waste.

Library of Congress Cataloging-in-Publication Data
Frederick, Shane.
The ultimate guide to pro hockey teams / by Shane Frederick.
    p. cm.—(Sports Illustrated KIDS. Ultimate Pro Guides)
  Includes index.
  ISBN 978-1-4296-4822-6 (library binding)
  ISBN 978-1-4296-5643-6 (paperback)
  1. Hockey—Juvenile literature. 2. Hockey teams—Juvenile literature.
  3. National Hockey League—Juvenile literature.
  I. Title. II. Series.
  GV847.25.F74 2011
  796.962'64—dc22   2010009999

Editorial Credits: Anthony Wacholtz, editor; Tracy Davies, designer;
Eric Gohl, media researcher; Laura Manthe, production specialist

Image Credits: Amy Berg, 35 (b); BigStockPhoto.com: Christopher Penler,
42 (t); Getty Images Inc.: Bruce Bennett Studios, 13 (t), Focus On Sport, 19
(t), NHL Images/Allsport/Glenn Cratty, 31 (b); iStockphoto: Dan Hauser
(hockey net), cover, Joseph Gareri (hockey rink), cover, back cover, 2, 3,
66–67, 68–69, 70, 72, Mark Stay (map), 68–69, Mikhail Kotov, cover (bl),
Stefan Klein (puck), cover, back cover, 1, 68; Newscom: 45 (b), 51 (t), 59
(t), AFP/Dan Levine, 57 (b), Icon SMI/Andy Altenburger, 23 (t), Icon SMI/
Jason Cohn, 65 (t), Icon SMI/Shelly Castellano, 15 (b), Icon SMI/Southcreek
Sports/Adrian Gauthier, 60 (b), Images Distribution, 61 (b), UPI Photo/
John Dickerson, 31 (t), Zuma Press/*The Sporting News*, 19 (b); Shutterstock:
doodle (shattered glass), back cover, 68, Rob Marmion, 4–5, Tomasz
Sowinski, design element; *Sports Illustrated*: Bob Rosato, 9 (t), 40 (b), 44 (b),
58 (all), 61 (t), 66 (background left), Damian Strohmeyer, 8 (all), 10 (t), 36
(t), 41 (t), 47 (t), 52 (b), 60 (t), 67 (front), David E. Klutho, cover (bm & br),
1, 6 (all), 7 (all), 10 (b), 12 (all), 13 (b), 14 (all), 15 (t), 16 (all), 17 (b), 18 (all),
20 (all), 21 (all), 22 (all), 23 (b), 24 (all), 25 (b), 26 (t), 27 (all), 28 (t), 29 (b),
30 (all), 32 (b), 33 (t), 34 (all), 35 (t), 38 (all), 39 (all), 40 (t), 41 (b), 46 (all),
47 (b), 48 (all), 50 (t), 52 (t), 53 (all), 54 (all), 56 (all), 57 (t), 59 (b), 62 (all),
63 (all), 66 (background middle & right), 67 (background all), Hy Peskin, 26
(b), 36 (b), 37 (b), John Biever, 28 (b), John D. Hanlon, 11 (b), 49 (all), John
G. Zimmerman, 44 (t), John Iacono, 42 (b), John W. McDonough, 32 (t),
Manny Millan, 17 (t), 43 (all), Robert Beck, 9 (b), 25 (t), 33 (b), 50 (b), 51 (b),
55 (all), 64 (b), 65 (b), 66 (front), Simon Bruty, 64 (t), Tony Triolo, 2, 11 (t),
29 (t), 37 (t), V.J. Lovero, 45 (t).

TABLE OF CONTENTS

THE GREATEST SHOW ON ICE

IN 1893 the Montreal AAA hockey club captured the Amateur Hockey Association's championship. Its prize for winning was a $50 silver bowl that was about 7 inches (18 centimeters) tall and 11 inches (28 cm) across. The trophy was donated by Sir Frederick Arthur Stanley, the governor general of Canada, who was better known as Lord Stanley of Preston. Today hockey teams are still playing for that trophy—the Stanley Cup.

The Cup is professional sports' oldest and most famous trophy. It has become the symbol of the National Hockey League (NHL). The trophy is unique because the roster of each

Franchise **records** are listed by wins, losses, **ties,** and overtime losses.

winning team is engraved on its base of rings. Also, each player from the winning team gets to keep the Cup for one day during the offseason. The trophy has been on boat rides, in parades, and at parties all around the world. Players have celebrated by drinking champagne out of the bowl. The players' kids have eaten ice cream from it. One player even bathed his newborn baby in the Cup.

Each season every team sets a goal of winning the Cup. Some have done it many times, while others have only come close. Skate through this book to see the teams and players who are hoping to be the next to lift the Stanley Cup.

All regular season stats are through the 2009–2010 season.

ANAHEIM DUCKS

Franchise Record: 557–539–107–77
Home Rink: Honda Center
(17,174 capacity) in Anaheim, California

STANLEY CUP
2007

First Season: 1993–1994

The Anaheim Ducks were all Hollywood when they joined the NHL. They were owned by the Walt Disney Company. They got their name—then called the Mighty Ducks of Anaheim—from a popular Disney hockey movie. The goalie even wore a mask that featured the face of cartoon character Donald Duck. But they are no joke. The Ducks have twice gone to the Stanley Cup finals and won it all in 2007.

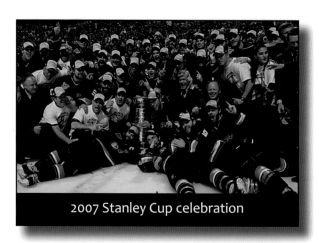
2007 Stanley Cup celebration

Legends & Stars

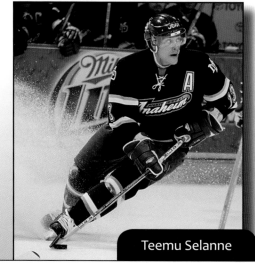
Teemu Selanne

Paul Kariya	LW	1994–2003	Two-time Lady Byng Trophy winner
Scott Niedermayer	D	2005–present	Longtime New Jersey Devil was a Conn Smythe winner with the Ducks
Teemu Selanne	RW	1996–2001, 2005–present	NHL's goal leader in 1999 has played in 10 All-Star Games

By the Numbers

TOP GOAL SCORER	**Teemu Selanne** 1996–2001, 2005–present 379 goals	**TOP GOALTENDER**	**Jean-Sebastien Giguere** 2000–2010 206 wins ⟶
TOP ASSISTS MAN	**Teemu Selanne** 412 assists	**TOP DEFENSEMAN**	**Scott Niedermayer** 2005–present 264 points

Consolation Prize

The Conn Smythe Trophy is awarded to the MVP of the Stanley Cup playoffs every year. A player on the losing team of the finals has won the award only five times in NHL history. Ducks goaltender Jean-Sebastien Giguere was one of those players. Although the Ducks fell to the Devils in Game 7 of the 2003 finals, Giguere's five shutouts in the playoffs earned him the award.

Rob (left) and Scott Niedermayer

Sibling Rivalry

Rob Niedermayer watched his older brother, Scott, lift the Stanley Cup with the New Jersey Devils three times. Rob never touched the trophy until Scott joined him on the Ducks. They won a title together in 2007.

ATLANTA THRASHERS

First Season: 1999–2000

Franchise Record: 308–401–45–66
Home Rink: Philips Arena
(18,750 capacity) in Atlanta, Georgia

STANLEY CUPS
None

The Atlanta Thrashers weren't the first NHL team to play in Georgia. Atlanta was the home of the Flames from 1972 to 1980 before the team packed up and moved to Calgary, Alberta, Canada. Nearly 20 years later, the NHL returned to Atlanta. Owners called the team the Thrashers, naming it after the Georgia state bird.

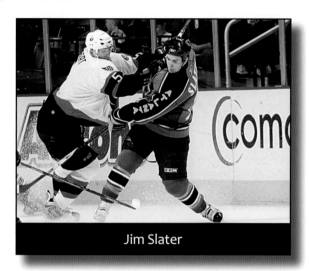
Jim Slater

Legends & Stars

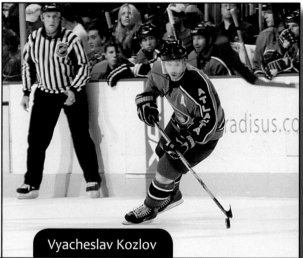
Vyacheslav Kozlov

Ilya Kovalchuk	LW	2001–2010	No. 1 overall draft pick in 2001 leads the team in scoring and assists
Vyacheslav Kozlov	LW	2002–present	Longtime Red Wings star had eight game-winning goals during the 2006–2007 season
Kari Lehtonen	G	2003–2009	Leads the Thrashers in career shutouts with 14

By the Numbers

TOP GOAL SCORER		TOP GOALTENDER	
Ilya Kovalchuk 2001–2010 328 goals		**Kari Lehtonen** 2003–2009 94 wins	

TOP ASSISTS MAN		TOP DEFENSEMAN	
Ilya Kovalchuk 287 assists		**Yannick Tremblay** 1999–2004 107 points	

Trophy Ceremony

Atlanta became the first team in the NHL's last expansion group to claim one of the league's prized player trophies. Winger Dany Heatley captured the Calder Trophy as rookie of the year in 2002.

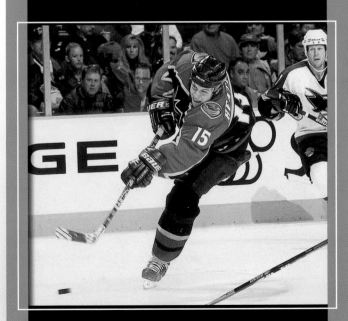

Dany Heatley

Dream Season

During the 2005–2006 season, the Thrashers enjoyed their first winning season (41–33–8). However, they didn't make the playoffs. That happened the next season, when they won two more games and became champions of the Southeast Division. Atlanta's lone playoff experience didn't last long, though. They were swept in the first round by the New York Rangers.

BOSTON BRUINS

First Season: 1924–1925

Franchise Record: 2,761–2,153–791–91
Home Rink: TD Banknorth Garden
(17,565 capacity) in Boston, Massachusetts

STANLEY CUPS
1929, 1939, 1941, 1970, 1972

The Boston Bruins were the first American team to join the Canadian-born NHL. Over their nearly 90 seasons, the B's have captured five Stanley Cups. One of the best players to ever lace up the skates was a Boston Bruin: the game-changing defenseman Bobby Orr.

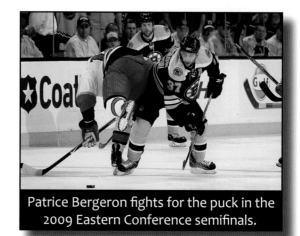

Patrice Bergeron fights for the puck in the 2009 Eastern Conference semifinals.

Legends & Stars

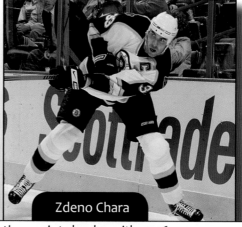

Zdeno Chara

Ray Bourque	D	1979–2000	Bruins all-time points leader with 1,506
Frank Brimsek	G	1938–1943, 1945–1949	"Mr. Zero" had 10 shutouts as a rookie; won two Cups
John Bucyk	LW	1957–1978	Played 21 seasons for the Bruins
Zdeno Chara	D	2006–present	Norris Trophy winner is the tallest player in the NHL
Phil Esposito	C	1967–1975	Led the league in scoring five times
Cam Neely	RW	1986–1996	Named to five All-Star Games
Bobby Orr	D	1966–1976	Won eight Norris, three Hart, and two Conn Smythe trophies
Art Ross		1924–1928, 1929–1934, 1936–1939, 1941–1945	Coached 16 seasons, winning 361 games and the 1939 Stanley Cup
Eddie Shore	D	1926–1939	Four-time Hart Trophy winner
Tim Thomas	G	2002–present	Won the Vezina and Jennings trophies in 2009

By the Numbers

Bobby Orr and Company

Defensemen don't always get the glory—unless they're playing for Boston. The Bruins have had some of the best defensemen to ever play the game. Bobby Orr is considered the best of all time. He changed the position, becoming the first defenseman to win a scoring title. Eddie Shore was a star in the sport's early days and won four MVPs. Ray Bourque is the top-scoring defenseman of all-time.

Bobby Orr (4) in the 1974 NHL playoffs

Breaking Down Barriers

On January 18, 1958, history was made when Bruins winger Willie O'Ree took the ice. O'Ree was the first black player to participate in an NHL game. The Fredericton, New Brunswick, Canada, native had a short professional career. He played in just two games that season and 43 games in 1960–1961. He scored four goals in 1958.

BUFFALO SABRES

First Season: 1970–1971

Franchise Record: 1,487–1,158–409–62

Home Rink: HSBC Arena
(18,690 capacity) in Buffalo, New York

STANLEY CUPS
None

When the NHL expanded for the first time after doubling the league in 1967, it added a team in Buffalo, New York. Buffalo had a successful minor-league hockey team for 30 years. The Sabres continued that success, reaching two Stanley Cup finals. However, they fell short of a championship each time, despite stars Gilbert Perreault and Dominik Hasek leading the way.

Sabres right wing Mike Grier (25)

Legends ★★★★ & Stars

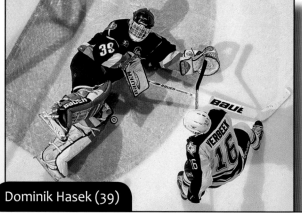
Dominik Hasek (39)

Dominik Hasek	G	1992–2001	Won both of his Hart trophies and six Vezina trophies while playing for Buffalo
Pat LaFontaine	C	1991–1997	Retired as the second-highest-scoring American-born player with 1,013 points
Rick Martin	LW	1971–1981	Selected to seven All-Star Games
Ryan Miller	G	2002–present	Selected to U.S. Olympic team in 2010
Gilbert Perreault	C	1970–1987	High-scoring forward won the Calder Trophy in 1971

By the Numbers

TOP GOAL SCORER	**Gilbert Perreault** 1970–1987 434 goals	**TOP GOALTENDER**	**Dominik Hasek** 1992–2001 234 wins
TOP ASSISTS MAN	**Gilbert Perreault** 814 assists	**TOP DEFENSEMAN**	**Phil Housley** 1982–1990 558 points

The French Connection

In the Sabres' early years, the trio of Gilbert Perreault, René Robert, and Rick Martin was a dominating forward line. Since they were all from French-speaking Quebec, the group was dubbed The French Connection. Their nickname was also the name of a popular movie at the time. The line led the Sabres to the 1975 finals, where they lost to the Philadelphia Flyers.

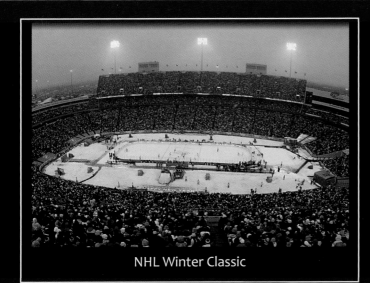

NHL Winter Classic

Outdoor Hockey

The first NHL Winter Classic, an annual New Year's Day outdoor game, took place in Buffalo's Ralph Wilson Stadium in 2008. The Sabres lost to the Pittsburgh Penguins in a shootout that snowy day. It was just the second regular-season outdoor game in NHL history.

CALGARY FLAMES

First Season: 1972–1973

Franchise Record: 1,359–1,156–379–66
Home Rink: Pengrowth Saddledome
(17,139 capacity) in Calgary, Alberta, Canada

STANLEY CUP
1989

David Moss

When the NHL expanded by two teams in 1972, the Canadian province of Alberta wasn't even considered. Instead, Atlanta was the choice, and the Flames were born. But after eight years and limited success, the team packed up and headed north to hockey country. In Calgary the Flames have played for three Stanley Cups, winning the prized trophy once.

Miikka Kiprusoff

Theoren Fleury	RW	1988–1998	Seven-time All-Star Game participant
Jarome Iginla	RW	1996–present	Led the NHL in scoring twice
Miikka Kiprusoff	G	2003–present	Awarded the Vezina Trophy in 2006
Al MacInnis	D	1981–1994	Won the Conn Smythe Trophy in 1989

By the Numbers

TOP GOAL SCORER	**Jarome Iginla** 1996–present 441 goals	**TOP GOALTENDER**	**Mike Vernon** 1982–1994, 2000–2002 262 wins
TOP ASSISTS MAN	**Al MacInnis** 1981–1994 609 assists	**TOP DEFENSEMAN**	**Al MacInnis** 822 points

Rare Win

The Flames captured the 1989 Stanley Cup by winning Game 6 of the finals. That game took place in Montreal, home of the mighty Canadiens. The win was significant because Flames veteran Lanny McDonald and his teammates became the first visiting team to celebrate a championship in the Canadiens' rink.

Calgary coach Darryl Sutter led the Flames to two playoff appearances.

All in the Family

The Sutter boys from tiny Viking, Alberta, are a hockey success story. Six brothers—Brent, Brian, Darryl, Duane, Rich, and Ron—all made it to the NHL. The Sutters have a close connection with the Flames. Ron played for the team, and Brent, Brian, and Darryl all coached it. Darryl led Calgary to the Cup finals in 2004. Two of the brothers' sons also played in the NHL. Darryl's son Brett debuted with the Flames in 2008–2009.

15

CAROLINA HURRICANES

First Season: 1979–1980

Franchise Record: 976–1,106–263–59

Home Rink: RBC Center
(18,730 capacity) in Raleigh, North Carolina

STANLEY CUP
2006

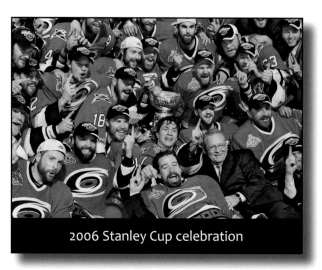
2006 Stanley Cup celebration

The Carolina Hurricanes' history goes back to another city and another league. They started as the New England Whalers of the World Hockey Association in 1972 and were one of four WHA teams to merge into the NHL in 1979. After spending 18 more seasons in Hartford, Connecticut, the team moved to Raleigh, North Carolina, in 1997 and became the Hurricanes.

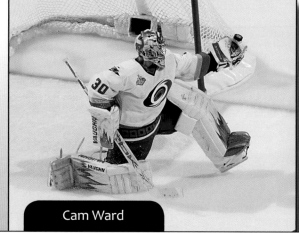
Cam Ward

Rod Brind'Amour	C	2000–present	Twice named the NHL's top defensive forward
Ron Francis	C	1981–1991, 1998–2004	Ranks second all-time in assists, third all-time in games played
Eric Staal	C	2003–present	Three-time All-Star Game pick
Cam Ward	G	2005–present	Won the Conn Smythe Trophy in 2006

By the Numbers

TOP GOAL SCORER	**Ron Francis** 1981–1991, 1998–2004 328 goals	**TOP GOALTENDER**	**Arturs Irbe** 1998–2004 130 wins
TOP ASSISTS MAN	**Ron Francis** 783 assists	**TOP DEFENSEMAN**	**Dave Babych** 1986–1991 240 points

And Howe (and Howe and Howe)

In 1977 the Whalers lured hockey legend Gordie Howe and his sons, defensemen Mark and Marty, to play for the team. They skated together for three seasons, including one year in the NHL when Gordie Howe was 51 years old. The longtime Red Wings star scored 15 goals and had 26 assists in his 32nd and final full year of professional hockey.

Eric Staal

Carolina Cup

The Hurricanes made it to the Stanley Cup finals in 2002, but they fell to the mighty Red Wings. Four years later, though, high-scoring center Eric Staal was skating the famous trophy around the rink after defeating the Edmonton Oilers. It was the state of North Carolina's first professional sports championship.

CHICAGO BLACKHAWKS

Franchise Record: 2,371–2,473–814–72
Home Rink: United Center
(20,500 capacity) in Chicago, Illinois

STANLEY CUPS
1934, 1938, 1961

First Season: 1926–1927

One of the NHL's "Original Six" teams, the Chicago Blackhawks were founded by coffee tycoon Major Frederic McLaughlin. To fill up his first roster, McLaughlin purchased Oregon's Portland Rosebuds of the Western Hockey League. Then he moved most of the players to the Windy City.

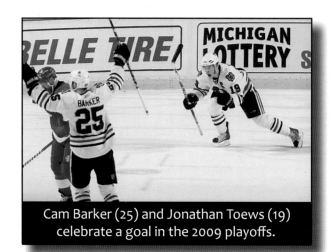

Cam Barker (25) and Jonathan Toews (19) celebrate a goal in the 2009 playoffs.

Legends & Stars

Patrick Kane

Chris Chelios	D	1990–1999	Won two of his three Norris trophies as a Blackhawk
Tony Esposito	G	1969–1984	Three-time Vezina Trophy winner and six-time All-Star
Glenn Hall	G	1957–1967	Three-time Vezina Trophy winner appeared in 502 consecutive games
Bobby Hull	LW	1957–1972	Won two Hart trophies and played in 12 All-Star Games
Patrick Kane	RW	2007–present	Won the Calder Trophy in 2008
Stan Mikita	C/RW	1958–1980	Two-time Hart and Lady Byng trophy winner
Pierre Pilote	D	1955–1968	Won the Norris Trophy three times in a row
Denis Savard	C	1980–1990, 1995–1997	Seven-time All-Star Game selection
Jonathan Toews	C	2007–present	All-Rookie pick was named captain in his second season

By the Numbers

TOP GOAL SCORER	**Bobby Hull** 1957–1972 604 goals	**TOP GOALTENDER**	**Tony Esposito** 1969–1984 418 wins	
TOP ASSISTS MAN	**Stan Mikita** 1958–1980 926 assists	**TOP DEFENSEMAN**	**Doug Wilson** 1977–1991 779 points	

Unlikely Championship

In 1938 the Blackhawks went 14–25–9 but managed to slip into the playoffs. Led by American goaltender Mike Karakas, Chicago upset the Montreal Canadiens and the New York Americans. Then they defeated the Toronto Maple Leafs in the Stanley Cup finals three games to one for their second championship.

Bobby Hull

The Golden Jet

In the late 1950s, a speedy, blond-haired left wing burst onto the ice for the Blackhawks. Bobby Hull, nicknamed "The Golden Jet" because of his yellow locks, could fire a slap shot up to 120 miles (193 kilometers) per hour. To make matters worse for goaltenders, he was one of the first players to add a curve to the blade of his stick, which made the puck fly unpredictably.

COLORADO AVALANCHE

First Season: 1979–1980

Franchise Record: 1,103–982–261–58
Home Rink: Pepsi Center
(18,007 capacity) in Denver, Colorado

STANLEY CUPS
1996, 2001

The NHL didn't last long its first time in Denver. In 1982 after just six years, the Colorado Rockies became the New Jersey Devils. But in 1995 another struggling franchise was on the move. The Quebec Nordiques, a World Hockey Association team that had merged into the NHL, moved west and became the Colorado Avalanche.

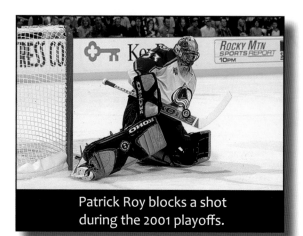

Patrick Roy blocks a shot during the 2001 playoffs.

Legends & Stars

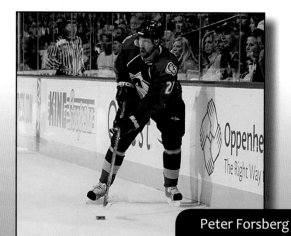

Peter Forsberg

Peter Forsberg	C	1994–2004, 2007–2008	Owns a Calder and a Hart trophy
Milan Hejduk	RW	1998–present	Led the NHL in goals in 2002–2003
Patrick Roy	G	1995–2003	Three-time Vezina Trophy winner ranks No. 2 on all-time wins list
Joe Sakic	C	1988–2009	1996 Conn Smythe winner and 2001 Hart Trophy winner
Paul Stastny	C	2006–present	Named to U.S. Olympic Team in 2010
Peter Stastny	C	1980–1990	Was the Nordiques' all-time leading scorer; still ranks second on the franchise list

By the Numbers

TOP GOAL SCORER	**Joe Sakic** 1988–2009 625 goals	**TOP GOALTENDER**	**Patrick Roy** 1995–2003 262 wins
TOP ASSISTS MAN	**Joe Sakic** 1,016 assists	**TOP DEFENSEMAN**	**Adam Foote** 1991–2004, 2008–present 251 points

Stastny Scores

In the early 1980s, three brothers from the country formerly known as Czechoslovakia—Peter, Anton, and Marian Stastny—went to Canada and played for the Quebec Nordiques. Peter became one of the top scorers not named Gretzky to skate in the NHL. The Nordiques retired Stastny's No. 26 jersey, but his son, Paul, now wears it for the Avs.

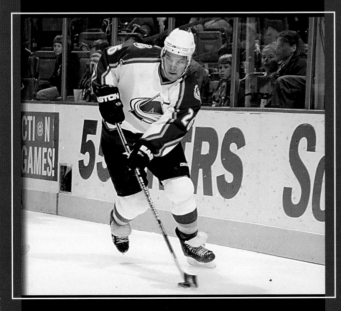

Paul Stastny

Ready to Win

In their last season in Quebec City, the Nordiques lost in the first round of the postseason. But with players such as Joe Sakic, Peter Forsberg, Valeri Kamensky, and Claude Lemieux, the franchise was ready for greatness. The next season the team had transformed into the Avalanche, traded for Hall-of-Fame goaltender Patrick Roy, and won the Stanley Cup.

COLUMBUS BLUE JACKETS

First Season: 2000–2001

Franchise Record: 279–360–33–66
Home Rink: Nationwide Arena
(18,138 capacity) in Columbus, Ohio

STANLEY CUPS
NONE

The second go-round of NHL hockey in Ohio has been more successful than the first. In 1976 the California Golden Seals moved to Cleveland and became known as the Barons. But that team lasted just two seasons before folding. More than 20 years later, Ohio's capital, Columbus, was awarded an expansion team, and the Blue Jackets were born.

Raffi Torres (14) controls the puck near the Red Wings' net during the 2009 playoffs.

Legends & Stars

Steve Mason (1)

Rostislav Klesla	D	2000–present	Selected to the NHL All-Rookie Team in 2001–2002
Steve Mason	G	2008–present	Calder Trophy winner and Vezina runner-up in 2009
Rick Nash	LW	2002–present	Four-time All-Star led the league in goals in 2004

By the Numbers

TOP GOAL SCORER
Rick Nash
2002–present
227 goals

TOP GOALTENDER
Marc Denis
2000–2006
84 wins

TOP ASSISTS MAN
David Vyborny
2000–2008
204 assists

TOP DEFENSEMAN
Rostislav Klesla
2000–present
123 points ⟶

Young Gun

Columbus made the right call picking Rick Nash with the No. 1 overall draft pick in 2002. By the end of the 2003–2004 season, the 19-year-old Nash was the youngest player in NHL history to lead the league in goals. He was also an All-Star that season, becoming the youngest to play in the game since 1986.

Rick Nash (61) won the Maurice Richard Trophy in 2003–2004.

Tragedy at the Rink

In 2002 Brittanie Cecil, a 13-year-old fan, was struck by a puck that had deflected into the stands at Nationwide Arena. She died two days later from the injury. She was the first fan to die in the 85-year history of the NHL. As a result the teams decided to hang netting behind the goals at all arenas to prevent such a tragedy from happening again.

DALLAS STARS

First Season: 1967–1968

Franchise Record: 1,426–1,393–459–64

Home Rink: American Airlines Center
(18,000 capacity) in Dallas, Texas

STANLEY CUP
1999

For 26 seasons the North Stars played in the Twin Cities of Minneapolis and St. Paul. But in 1993 the team moved to Texas, dropped the word North from its name, and became the Dallas Stars. In Minnesota the Stars went to two Stanley Cup finals, but they finally won a title in Dallas in 1999.

Brett Hull (22) takes a shot against the Colorado Avalanche during the 1999 playoffs.

Legends & Stars

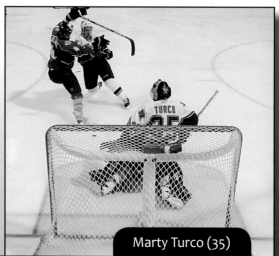

Marty Turco (35)

Ed Belfour	G	1997–2002	Allowed the fewest goals in the NHL four times
Neal Broten	C	1980–1995, 1996–1997	Team's all-time leading scorer during the Minnesota years
Mike Modano	C	1989–present	Named to seven All-Star Games in 20 years with the Stars
Joe Nieuwendyk	C	1995–2002	Conn Smythe Trophy winner in 1999
Marty Turco	G	2000–present	Three-time All-Star Game selection

By the Numbers

TOP GOAL SCORER	**Mike Modano** 1989–present 557 goals	**TOP GOALTENDER**	**Marty Turco** 2000–present 262 wins
TOP ASSISTS MAN	**Mike Modano** 802 assists	**TOP DEFENSEMAN**	**Sergei Zubov** 1996–2009 549 points

Epic Win

When Brett Hull scored the Stanley Cup-clinching goal in the third overtime of Game 6 in the 1999 finals, it was the end of a marathon night. The Stars and the Sabres battled for 114 minutes, 51 seconds and combined for 104 shots on goal. Dallas goalie Ed Belfour made 53 saves in the 2-1 Stars victory.

Stars right wing Pat Verbeek (16) fights for the puck during the 1999 Stanley Cup Finals.

American Hero

The Minnesota North Stars drafted Mike Modano with the No. 1 overall pick in 1988. In 2010 the talented center was in his 20th season with the franchise. The Michigan native didn't just become the Stars' all-time leading scorer, he became the top-scoring American-born NHL player, recording more than 1,350 points.

DETROIT RED WINGS

First Season: 1926–1927

Franchise Record: 2,616–2,231–815–68

Home Rink: Joe Louis Arena
(20,066 capacity) in Detroit, Michigan

STANLEY CUPS
1936, 1937, 1943, 1950, 1952, 1954, 1955, 1997, 1998, 2002, 2008

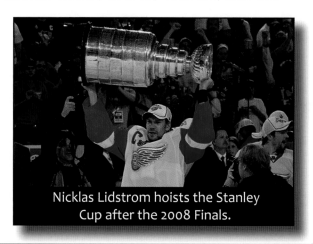

Nicklas Lidstrom hoists the Stanley Cup after the 2008 Finals.

With 11 NHL championships—more than any other hockey team in the United States—Detroit earned the nickname "Hockeytown." Only the Canadiens and the Maple Leafs have more Stanley Cup wins. First known as the Detroit Cougars and then the Falcons, the team became the Red Wings in 1932.

Legends & Stars

Terry Sawchuk

Jack Adams		1927–1947	Wings' second coach won three championships in 20 years
Alex Delvecchio	C/LW	1950–1974	Named to the All-Star Game 13 times in 24 seasons
Sergei Fedorov	C	1990–2003	Won the Hart Trophy once and the Frank J. Selke Trophy twice
Gordie Howe	RW	1946–1971	Six-time Hart Trophy winner ranks third on the all-time points list
Red Kelly	D	1947–1960	Captured four Lady Byng awards and one Norris Trophy
Nicklas Lidstrom	D	1991–present	Owns six Norris trophies and one Conn Smythe Trophy
Ted Lindsay	LW	1944–1957, 1964–1965	Captained three Stanley Cup winners in the 1950s
Chris Osgood	G	1993–2001, 2005–present	Two-time Jennings Trophy winner
Terry Sawchuk	G	1949–1955, 1957–1964, 1968–1969	Four-time Vezina Trophy winner
Steve Yzerman	C	1983–2006	1998 Conn Smythe winner played 22 seasons in Detroit

By the Numbers

TOP GOAL SCORER	Gordie Howe 1946–1971 786 goals	TOP GOALTENDER	Terry Sawchuk 1949–1955, 1957–1964, 1968–1969, 351 wins
TOP ASSISTS MAN	Steve Yzerman 1983–2006 1,063 assists	TOP DEFENSEMAN	Nicklas Lidstrom 1991–present 1,046 points

Mr. Hockey

There's a reason Gordie Howe got the nickname "Mr. Hockey": He could do it all. In more than 25 seasons in Detroit, Howe led the league in scoring six times. In 14 other seasons, he ranked among the top five and finished his NHL career with 1,850 points and four championships.

Throwing the Octopus

A slimy tradition started in 1952. That's when a dead octopus was first thrown onto the ice during a Red Wings home playoff game for good luck. The creature's eight legs then represented the eight wins a team needed to win the Stanley Cup. Even though more games are now needed, the smelly tradition continues.

EDMONTON OILERS

First Season: 1979–1980

Franchise Record: 1,119–951–262–72

Home Rink: Rexall Place (16,839 capacity) in Edmonton, Alberta, Canada

STANLEY CUPS
1984, 1985, 1987, 1988, 1990

One of four World Hockey Association teams to join the NHL, the Edmonton Oilers became a dynasty in the 1980s, thanks to "The Great One"—Wayne Gretzky. The superstar and his high-flying, high-scoring supporting cast scored 400 goals a season five years in a row. That run included an NHL-record 446 goals over 80 games (5.6 per game) during the Alberta team's first Stanley Cup season in 1983–1984.

Coach Craig MacTavish won more than 300 games in eight seasons with the Oilers.

Legends & Stars

Shawn Horcoff

Glenn Anderson	RW	1980–1991, 1996	Four-time All-Star Game selection
Paul Coffey	D	1980–1987	Three-time Norris Trophy winner and a 14-time All-Star Game pick
Grant Fuhr	G	1981–1991	Won the Vezina Trophy in 1988
Wayne Gretzky	C	1978–1988	NHL's all-time leading scorer won nine Hart trophies in 10 years
Shawn Horcoff	C	2000–present	2008 All-Star Game pick
Jari Kurri	RW	1980–1990	Ranks second on the Oilers' all-time scoring list
Mark Messier	C	1979–1991	Two-time MVP ranks second on the NHL's all-time points list
Glen Sather		1976–1989, 1993–1994	Edmonton coach led the Oilers to four Stanley Cup championships

By the Numbers

TOP GOAL SCORER	**Wayne Gretzky** 1978–1988 583 goals	**TOP GOALTENDER**	**Grant Fuhr** 1981–1991 266 wins
TOP ASSISTS MAN	**Wayne Gretzky** 1,086 assists	**TOP DEFENSEMAN**	**Paul Coffey** 1980–1987 669 points

How Great?

It's safe to say that Wayne Gretzky's records will never be broken. Number 99 was the only player to score more than 200 points in a season. He accomplished the feat four times, including a record 215-point performance (52 goals, 163 assists) in 1985–1986. Gretzky scored a record 92 goals in 1981–1982. His career-points mark of 2,857 includes 1,963 assists, which is more than the total points compiled by anyone else who's ever played.

Mess and the Rest

If people needed proof that the Oilers were more than just Wayne Gretzky, they got it in 1990. Two years after Gretzky was traded to the Kings, Edmonton won another Stanley Cup. That team included captain Mark Messier and six others who were part of all five of the Oilers' championships.

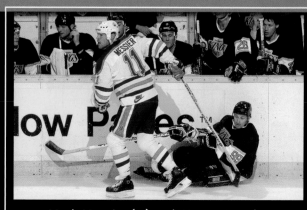

Mark Messier (11) and Wayne Gretzky

FLORIDA PANTHERS

First Season: 1993–1994

Franchise Record: 505–539–142–94
Home Rink: BankAtlantic Center
(19,250 capacity) in Sunrise, Florida

STANLEY CUPS
None

To say that the Panthers burst onto the NHL scene would be an understatement. The expansion team from south Florida was the most successful first-year team in league history, winning 33 games and compiling 83 points for the Atlantic Division standings in 1993–1994. Two years later the Panthers were competing for the Stanley Cup.

Jay Bouwmeester (4) was selected to the 2007 and 2009 All-Star games.

Legends & Stars

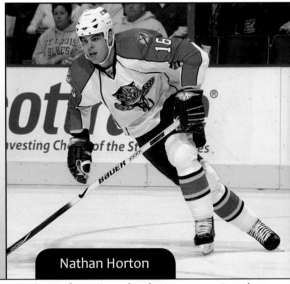
Nathan Horton

Pavel Bure	RW	1998–2002	Led the NHL in goals twice—both times as a Panther
Nathan Horton	C	2003–present	No. 3 overall draft pick in 2003
John Vanbiesbrouck	G	1993–1998	1986 Vezina Trophy winner's three All-Star seasons were in Florida
Stephen Weiss	C	2001–present	No. 4 overall draft pick in 2001

By the Numbers

TOP GOAL SCORER	Olli Jokinen 2000–2009 188 goals	TOP GOALTENDER	Roberto Luongo 2000–2006 108 wins
TOP ASSISTS MAN	Olli Jokinen 231 assists	TOP DEFENSEMAN	Robert Svehla 1994–2002 290 points

Tough Out

The Panthers were swept by the Colorado Avalanche in the 1996 Stanley Cup finals, but they didn't go down without a fight. Game 4 was scoreless into the third overtime before the Avs scored to clinch the title.

Rat Trick

On opening night of the 1995-1996 season, a rat scurried across the floor of the Panthers' locker room. Forward Scott Mellanby killed it with a slap shot against the wall. That night Mellanby scored two goals, and goalie John Vanbiesbrouck proclaimed it hockey's first "rat trick." The legend was born. As the season went on, fans threw rubber rats on the ice after Florida's first goal of a game. By the time the Stanley Cup finals came along, more than 2,000 fake rats were thrown onto the ice each game.

31

LOS ANGELES KINGS

First Season: 1967–1968

The NHL's "Original Six" teams all resided in cold-weather cities. But when the league made its first big expansion, it went to sunny southern California, and the Los Angeles Kings were born. Although the Kings have never won a title, they have had some of the most electric offensive players wear their uniform, including Marcel Dionne and Wayne Gretzky.

Franchise Record: 1,342–1,504–424–72

Home Rink: Staples Center
(18,118 capacity) in Los Angeles, California

STANLEY CUPS
None

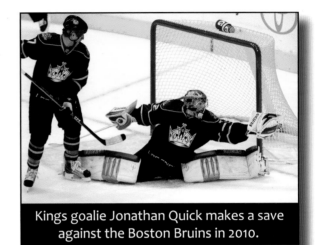

Kings goalie Jonathan Quick makes a save against the Boston Bruins in 2010.

Legends & Stars

Drew Doughty

Rob Blake	D	1989–2001, 2006–2008	Norris Trophy winner in 1998
Marcel Dionne	C	1975–1987	Ranks fifth on the NHL's all-time scoring list
Drew Doughty	D	2008–present	Second overall draft pick in 2008 and All-Rookie Team pick in 2009
Wayne Gretzky	C	1988–1996	"The Great One" led the NHL in scoring and won one Hart Trophy as a King
Luc Robitaille	LW	1986–2001, 2003–2006	Eight-time All-Star Game pick and Calder Trophy winner

By the Numbers

TOP GOAL SCORER
Luc Robitaille
1986–2001,
2003–2006
557 goals

TOP GOALTENDER
Rogie Vachon
1971–1978
171 wins

TOP ASSISTS MAN
Marcel Dionne
1975–1987
757 assists

TOP DEFENSEMAN
Rob Blake →
1989–2001,
2006–2008
494 points

Down but Not Out

Six years before getting "The Great One," the Kings pulled off the unthinkable. They eliminated Gretzky's Oilers from the Stanley Cup playoffs. The series win included a stunning, come-from-behind victory. The Kings were down 5-0 after two periods, but they came back to win 6-5 in overtime.

Trade of the Century

August 9, 1988, is a date that changed the NHL forever. That's when the Edmonton Oilers traded the game's greatest player, Wayne Gretzky, to the Los Angeles Kings. Number 99—now retired by the entire league—played to sellout crowds every night. He led L.A. to its only Stanley Cup finals appearance. After winning four times with the Oilers, however, he couldn't clinch one for the Kings.

Each Kings player wore Gretzky's 99 as a tribute after his number was retired.

MINNESOTA WILL

Franchise Record: 331–291–55–61

Home Rink: Xcel Energy Center
(18,834 capacity) in St. Paul, Minnesota

STANLEY CUPS
None

First Season: 2000–2001

Minnesota is the self-proclaimed "State of Hockey." But after the North Stars left for Dallas in 1993, the state was without an NHL team for seven years. When the league expanded for the last time, it was only natural to go back to a hockey-crazy part of the United States. In 2010 the team played in its 400th home game. Every one of those games was played before a sellout crowd, the third-longest sellout streak in NHL history.

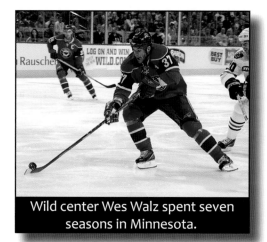

Wild center Wes Walz spent seven seasons in Minnesota.

Legends & Stars

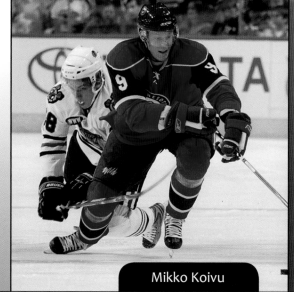
Mikko Koivu

Niklas Backstrom	G	2006–present	Jennings Trophy winner in 2007
Marian Gaborik	RW	2000–2009	Two-time All-Star Game selection
Mikko Koivu	C	2005–present	Wild captain was a first-round draft pick in 2001

By the Numbers

TOP GOAL SCORER	**Marian Gaborik** 2000–2009 219 goals	
TOP GOALTENDER	**Niklas Backstrom** 2006–present 119 wins ⟶	
TOP ASSISTS MAN	**Marian Gaborik** 218 assists	
TOP DEFENSEMAN	**Brent Burns** 2003–present 137 points	

Playoff Run

In just its third season in the NHL, the Wild made a playoff charge all the way to the Western Conference finals. The unlikely run included overtime victories in Games 6 and 7 against the favored Colorado Avalanche. Andrew Brunette's series-winning goal not only led his team to the second round, it also ended the career of goaltending great Patrick Roy, who retired after the season.

Fans Are Number 1

The Minnesota Wild team is too new to have retired numbers. However, the team quickly paid tribute to its fans by raising the number 1 to the ceiling of the Xcel Energy Center.

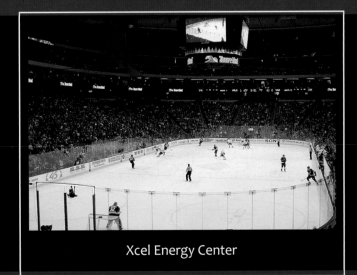

Xcel Energy Center

35

MONTREAL CANADIENS

First Season: 1917–1918

Franchise Record: 3,060–1,987–837–72

Home Rink: Bell Centre
(22,500 capacity) in Montreal, Quebec, Canada

STANLEY CUPS

1916, 1924, 1930, 1931, 1944, 1946,
1953, 1956, 1957, 1958, 1959, 1960,
1965, 1966, 1968, 1969, 1971, 1973,
1976, 1977, 1978, 1979, 1986, 1993

When it comes to winning, few sports teams have had the success of the Montreal Canadiens. With 24 Stanley Cup victories, only Major League Baseball's New York Yankees have won more championships (27). Twice, the nearly century-old hockey club won four titles in a row, a feat accomplished just one other time in NHL history.

Canadiens defenseman Josh Gorges controls the puck in the 2009 playoffs.

Legends & Stars

Jacques Plante

Jean Beliveau	C	1950–1951, 1952–1971	Won 10 Stanley Cups, including five as team captain
Hector "Toe" Blake		1955–1968	Montreal coach led Canadiens to eight championships
Scotty Bowman		1971–1979	Canadiens coach won five of his nine Stanley Cups with Montreal
Ken Dryden	G	1970–1979	Won the Calder and Conn Smythe trophies as a rookie
Doug Harvey	D	1947–1961	Seven-time Norris Trophy winner
Guy Lafleur	RW	1971–1985	Led the league in scoring three times; won five Cups
Howie Morenz	C	1923–1934, 1936–1937	One of the NHL's first stars was a three-time Hart Trophy winner
Jacques Plante	G	1952–1963	Seven-time Vezina Trophy winner was the first goalie to wear a mask
Carey Price	C	2007–present	First-round draft pick was the All-Rookie Team goalie in 2008
Maurice Richard	RW	1942–1960	"Rocket" led the Canadiens to eight Stanley Cup victories
Larry Robinson	D	1972–1989	Conn Smythe Trophy winner in 1976

By the Numbers

TOP GOAL SCORER	**Maurice Richard** 1942–1960 544 goals	**TOP GOALTENDER**	**Jacques Plante** 1952–1963 314 wins
TOP ASSISTS MAN	**Guy Lafleur** 1971–1985 728 assists	**TOP DEFENSEMAN**	**Larry Robinson** 1972–1989 883 points

Riot for the Rocket

Maurice "Rocket" Richard, a fan favorite, was suspended for the rest of the 1955 season after injuring an opposing player and punching an official. After learning about Richard's suspension, people rioted in the streets of Montreal, causing $500,000 in damage. In 1957 Richard became the NHL's first 500-goal scorer.

Maurice Richard scores against Red Wings goalie Terry Sawchuk during a 1954 game.

The Canadiens' Cup

With 24 championships, the Stanley Cup has belonged to Montreal for nearly a quarter of its history. Jean Beliveau has his name on the Cup 17 times—10 as a player and seven as a team executive. Henri Richard, brother of Maurice Richard, won it 11 times as a player—more than any other. Yvan Cournoyer also has his name on it 10 times.

NASHVILLE PREDATORS

Franchise Record: 411–371–60–60
Home Rink: Bridgestone Arena
(17,113 capacity) in Nashville, Tennessee

STANLEY CUPS
None

First Season: 1998–1999

In 1971 construction workers in downtown Nashville discovered an underground cave. A 9-inch (23-centimeter) fang and a leg bone of a saber-toothed tiger were found in the cave. Nearly 30 years later, the NHL arrived in Tennessee. Instead of naming the new team after Nashville's famous country-music scene, it was called the Predators and the logo became an ancient tiger.

Predators goalie Pekka Rinne had seven shutouts during the 2009–2010 season.

Legends & Stars

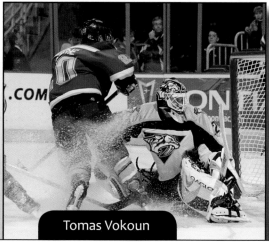

Tomas Vokoun

Jason Arnott	C	2006–present	Two-time All-Star Game participant
Steve Sullivan	RW	2004–present	Bill Masterton Trophy winner in 2009
Tomas Vokoun	G	1998–2007	Named to the All-Star Game twice as a Predator

By the Numbers

TOP GOAL SCORER	**David Legwand** 1998–present 152 goals	
TOP ASSISTS MAN	**David Legwand** 255 assists	
TOP GOALTENDER	**Tomas Vokoun** 1998–2007 161 wins	
TOP DEFENSEMAN	**Kimmo Timonen** 1998–2007 301 points	

Perfect Marriage

Many expansion teams go through several coaches and managers before getting things right. Not Nashville. Since the Predators first took the ice in 1998, general manager David Poile and head coach Barry Trotz have been running the team.

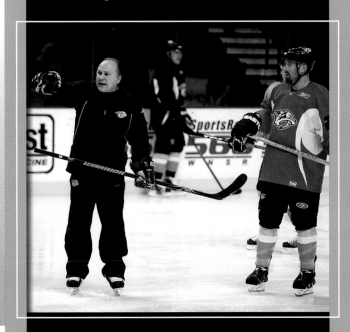

Predators coach Barry Trotz (left)

Historic Skate

On opening night of the 2003–2004 season, Predators rookie Jordin Tootoo became the first player of Inuit descent to appear in an NHL game. Tootoo was raised in Rankin Inlet, Nunavut, in northern Canada. Tootoo played five seasons in the NHL, all with Nashville, and had 26 goals and 35 assists.

NEW JERSEY DEVILS

First Season: 1974–1975

Franchise Record: 1,174–1,246–328–56
Home Rink: Prudential Center
(17,625 capacity) in Newark, New Jersey

STANLEY CUPS
1995, 2000, 2003

The Devils started out in the Midwest as the Kansas City Scouts. Two years later, in 1976, they moved west and became the Colorado Rockies. But the team finally found a home on the East Coast in 1982. In New Jersey the team enjoyed its first winning season, its first playoff series win, and three Stanley Cup championships.

Martin Brodeur proudly displays the Stanley Cup after the 2003 Finals.

Legends & Stars

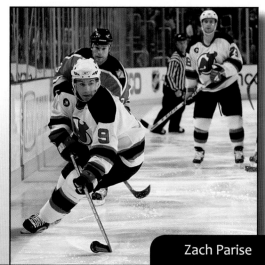

Zach Parise

Martin Brodeur	G	1991–present	Four-time Vezina Trophy winner
Ken Daneyko	D	1983–2003	Played in a team-record 1,283 games over 20 seasons
Claude Lemieux	F	1990–1995	Conn Smythe Trophy winner in 1995
Zach Parise	LW	2005–present	High-scoring forward earned his first All-Star selection in 2009
Scott Stevens	D	1991–2004	Tough body checker led the Devils to three titles

By the Numbers

TOP GOAL SCORER
John MacLean
1983–1997
347 goals

TOP GOALTENDER
Martin Brodeur
1991–present
602 wins

TOP ASSISTS MAN
Patrick Elias
1995–2009
411 assists

TOP DEFENSEMAN
Scott Niedermayer
1991–2004
476 points

All-Time Winner

In 2009 the Devils' Martin Brodeur won his 552nd game. He became the winningest goaltender in NHL history, passing Patrick Roy. At that point he also had 100 career shutouts—just three shy of Terry Sawchuk's record. Brodeur has won the William M. Jennings Trophy for allowing the fewest goals in a season.

Devils goalie Martin Brodeur

Comeback Kids

To win the 2000 Stanley Cup, the Devils did something no other team had done. They were down three games to one in the conference finals, but they came back to beat the Flyers. They went on to defeat the Stars for the title.

NEW YORK ISLANDERS

First Season: 1972–1973

Franchise Record: 1,283–1,269–347–61
Home Rink: Nassau Veterans Memorial Coliseum
(16,234 capacity) in Uniondale, New York

STANLEY CUPS
1980, 1981, 1982, 1983

The New York Islanders were the team of the early 1980s. In that era the team representing Long Island won four consecutive Stanley Cups. Only one other franchise in NHL history had ever accomplished that feat—the Montreal Canadiens did it twice.

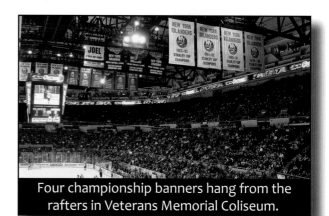

Four championship banners hang from the rafters in Veterans Memorial Coliseum.

Legends & Stars

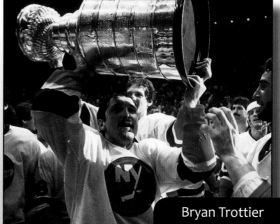

Bryan Trottier

Al Arbour		1973–1986, 1988–1994, 2007	Coached New York's four championship teams
Mike Bossy	RW	1977–1987	Scored a record 53 goals as a rookie
Clark Gillies	LW	1974–1986	Scored 30 or more goals in six different seasons
Denis Potvin	D	1973–1988	Captain of the Islanders' four title teams
Billy Smith	G	1972–1989	Conn Smythe Trophy winner in 1983
John Tavares	C	2009–present	No. 1 overall draft pick in 2009
Bryan Trottier	C	1975–1990	Retired as the NHL's sixth all-time leading scorer

By the Numbers

TOP GOAL SCORER	**Mike Bossy** 1977–1987 573 goals	**TOP GOALTENDER**	**Billy Smith** 1972–1989 304 wins
TOP ASSISTS MAN	**Bryan Trottier** 1975–1990 853 assists	**TOP DEFENSEMAN**	**Denis Potvin** 1973–1988 742 assists

Working Overtime

On their way to their first Stanley Cup, the Islanders won six of seven overtime games in the playoffs. That included Game 6 of the finals against the Philadelphia Flyers. Bobby Nystrom scored the game-winning goal to give the Islanders the championship.

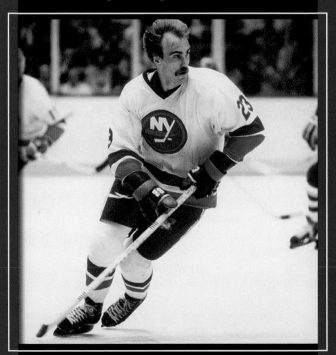

Bobby Nystrom

Easter Epic

In 1987 the Isles won a playoff game that started on a Saturday night in April and didn't end until early Easter Sunday morning. New York's Pat LaFontaine scored during the fourth overtime to clinch the victory. It was the NHL's first four-overtime game in 36 years.

NEW YORK RANGERS

Franchise Record: 2,440–2,407–808–75
Home Rink: Madison Square Garden
(18,200 capacity) in New York, New York

STANLEY CUPS
1928, 1933, 1940, 1994

First Season: 1926–1927

The Rangers weren't the first NHL team to play at Madison Square Garden, but they were the survivors. In 1926 the New York Americans also called Manhattan home. But the Rangers, nicknamed the Blueshirts, quickly became the top team in the league. They earned the best record in the league in their first year and clinched the Stanley Cup in their second.

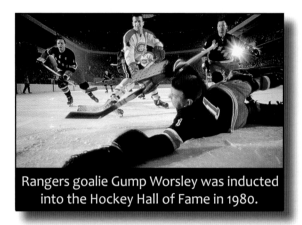

Rangers goalie Gump Worsley was inducted into the Hockey Hall of Fame in 1980.

Legends & Stars

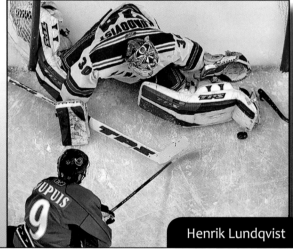

Henrik Lundqvist

Andy Bathgate	RW	1952–1964	NHL's MVP in 1959
Frank Boucher	C	1926–1938, 1943–1944	Seven-time Lady Byng Trophy winner
Bill Cook	RW	1926–1937	Captain of the Rangers' first two championship teams
Brian Leetch	D	1987–2003	Won two Norris trophies and the Conn Smythe in 1994
Henrik Lundqvist	G	2005–present	All-Rookie goalie in 2006
Brad Park	D	1968–1975	Named to nine All-Star Games in 17 seasons
Lester Patrick		1926–1939	The Rangers' first coach won two Stanley Cups

By the Numbers

TOP GOAL SCORER
Rod Gilbert
1960–1978
406 goals

TOP GOALTENDER
Mike Richter
1989–2003
301 wins

TOP ASSISTS MAN
Brian Leetch
1987–2003
741 assists

TOP DEFENSEMAN
Brian Leetch ⟶
981 points

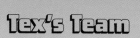

1940 Chant

For many years opposing fans mocked the Rangers by chanting "1940! 1940!" during playoff games. That was the last year they had won a title. But captain Mark Messier put an end to the chant in 1994, helping New York hoist the Stanley Cup again.

Mark Messier was inducted into the NHL Hall of Fame in 2007.

Tex's Team

The Rangers were first organized by Madison Square Garden President G.I. "Tex" Rickard. While the team was being formed, sportswriters had fun with Rickard's nickname. They called the team Tex's Rangers—playing off the name of the famous lawmen, the Texas Rangers. Rickard liked the name so much he had it stitched on the team's jerseys.

OTTAWA SENATORS

First Season: 1992–1993

Franchise Record: 606–580–115–63
Home Rink: Scotiabank Place
(20,004 capacity) in Ottawa, Ontario, Canada

STANLEY CUPS
None

For the first 34 years of the 1900s, the Ottawa Senators played professional hockey and even won the Stanley Cup. But the team folded in 1934, leaving Canada's hockey-hungry capital city without an NHL team for almost 60 years. When the league expanded in 1992, a new team with an old name was formed.

Senators goalie Brian Elliott

Legends & Stars

Dany Heatley

Daniel Alfredsson	RW	1995–present	Calder Trophy winner in 1996
Dany Heatley	LW	2003–2009	Had two 100-point seasons for the Senators
Jason Spezza	C	2002–present	Drafted second overall in 2001

By the Numbers

TOP GOAL SCORER	TOP GOALTENDER
Daniel Alfredsson 1995–present 375 goals	**Patrick Lalime** 1999–2004 146 wins

TOP ASSISTS MAN	TOP DEFENSEMAN
Daniel Alfredsson 616 assists	**Wade Redden** 1996–2008 410 points

Captain Dan

Since he was drafted in 1994 and joined the Senators in 1995, Daniel Alfredsson has been the face of the franchise. Fittingly, he has worn the captain's "C" since 1999. He also scored the overtime game-winning goal to put Ottawa into the Stanley Cup finals in 2007. They ended up losing the series to the Anaheim Ducks.

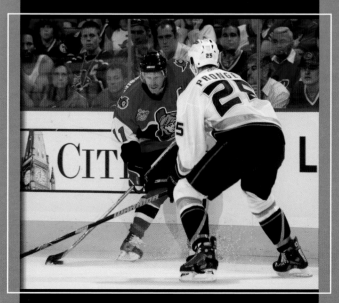

Daniel Alfredsson (11)

Tribute to the Past

During their franchise-opening game, the Senators paid tribute to the city's original team. They retired the number 8, the jersey number of Frank Finnigan. He led the old Senators to a 1927 Stanley Cup championship. In his later years, Finnigan campaigned to bring the NHL back to Ottawa.

47

PHILADELPHIA FLYERS

Franchise Record: 1,662–1,153–457–70
Home Rink: Wachovia Center
(19,519 capacity) in Philadelphia, Pennsylvania

STANLEY CUPS
1974, 1975

First Season: 1967–1968

In 1967 the NHL expanded from six teams to 12, adding franchises in California, Minnesota, Missouri, and Pennsylvania. One of those Pennsylvania teams, the Philadelphia Flyers, became the first of the new teams to win the Stanley Cup. They won back-to-back titles in their flashy, orange sweaters in the mid-1970s.

The Philadelphia Flyers took on the Boston Bruins in the 2010 NHL Winter Classic.

Legends & Stars

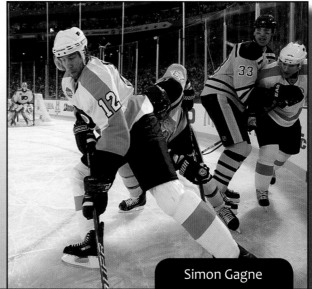

Simon Gagne

Bill Barber	LW	1972–1984	Played in six All-Star Games
Bobby Clarke	C	1969–1984	Three-time Hart Trophy winner
Simon Gagne	LW	1999–present	All-Rookie in 2000 and two-time All-Star Game pick
Eric Lindros	C	1992–2000	Hart Trophy winner in 1995
Bernie Parent	G	1967–1971, 1973–1979	Conn Smythe Trophy winner in each Stanley Cup run
Fred Shero		1971–1978	Coached the Flyers to their two championships

By the Numbers

TOP GOAL SCORER	**Bill Barber** 1972–1984 420 goals	**TOP GOALTENDER**	**Ron Hextall** 1986–1992, 1994–1999 240 wins
TOP ASSISTS MAN	**Bobby Clarke** 1969–1984 852 assists	**TOP DEFENSEMAN**	**Mark Howe** 1982–1992 342 assists

Broad Street Bullies

There wasn't anything fancy about the Flyers' title teams. Captain Bobby Clarke's squad knew how to win ugly games, often intimidating and fighting their opponents. Since their home arena, the Spectrum, was located on Broad Street, the feisty team was given the nickname the Broad Street Bullies.

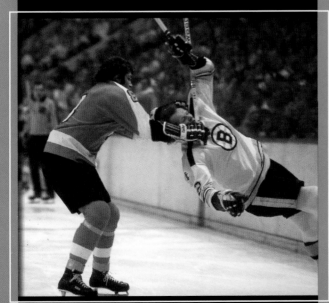

Flyers left wing Dave Schultz (left) makes a hard check in the 1974 NHL Finals.

Hextall Shoots and Scores

Goaltender Ron Hextall did a lot more than stop pucks. He was considered one of the best puck-handling and passing goalies in the league. On December 8, 1987, Hextall did something no other goaltender had ever done before: shoot and score a goal. It happened late in the game after the Boston Bruins had pulled their goalie for an extra skater. Hextall got the puck and fired it the length of the ice into the empty net. He did it again on April 11, 1989, becoming the first goalie to score in a playoff game.

PHOENIX COYOTES

First Season: 1979–1980

Franchise Record: 978–1,105–266–55
Home Rink: Jobing.com Arena
(17,653 capacity) in Glendale, Arizona

STANLEY CUPS
None

In 1979 the four remaining World Hockey Association teams merged into the NHL. One of those was the Winnipeg Jets, a three-time WHA champion led by former NHL superstar Bobby Hull. The Jets were the WHA's last title winner. The team played 17 seasons in Manitoba, Canada, before leaving in 1996 for the American desert and becoming the Phoenix Coyotes.

Coyotes right wing Shane Doan was selected to two All-Star Games.

Legends & Stars

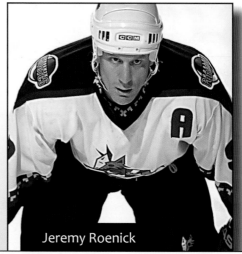

Jeremy Roenick

Shane Doan	RW	1995–present	Original Coyote played in two All-Star Games
Dale Hawerchuk	C	1981–1990	1982 Calder Trophy winner played nine seasons with the Jets
Teppo Numminen	D	1988–2003	Three-time All-Star selection played 15 seasons with the Jets/Coyotes
Jeremy Roenick	C	1996–2001, 2006–2007	Nine-time All-Star Game selection
Keith Tkachuk	LW	1991–2001	Five-time All-Star pick played in Winnipeg and Phoenix

By the Numbers

TOP GOAL SCORER
Dale Hawerchuk
1981–1990
379 goals

TOP GOALTENDER
Bob Essensa
1988–1994,
1999–2000
129 wins

TOP ASSISTS MAN
Thomas Steen
1981–1995
553 assists

TOP DEFENSEMAN
Teppo Numminen
1988–2003
534 points

Zero Tolerance

In 2004 Coyotes goaltender Brian Boucher broke what many thought would be an untouchable record. He set the modern record for consecutive shutouts, blanking teams in five straight games. He kept the puck out of his goal for 332 minutes, 1 second.

Gretzky Joins the Team

Wayne Gretzky played for the Oilers, Kings, Blues, and Rangers. He took on a different role with the Coyotes, becoming a partial owner in 2000. He was also put in charge of managing the hockey team. In 2005 he named himself the team's head coach. Gretzky coached for four seasons, winning 143 games.

PITTSBURGH PENGUINS

Franchise Record: 1,407–1,480–383–72

Home Rink: Consol Energy Center
(18,087 capacity) in Pittsburgh, Pennsylvania

STANLEY CUPS
1991, 1992, 2009

First Season: 1967–1968

Few teams get to say they have one of the greatest players of all time in their uniform. For the Pittsburgh Penguins, it was "Super" Mario Lemieux, who led the team to back-to-back championships in the early 1990s. The Penguins are now able to boast of another star: Sidney Crosby. The young phenom took the Penguins to a title in 2009 and scored the game-winning goal for Canada in the 2010 Winter Olympics.

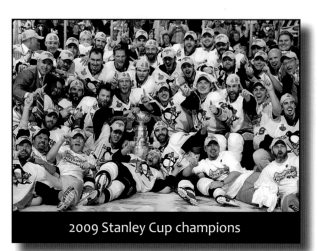

2009 Stanley Cup champions

Legends & Stars

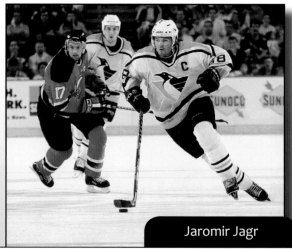

Jaromir Jagr

Sidney Crosby	C	2005–present	2007 Hart Trophy winner led Penguins to their third Cup
Ron Francis	C	1991–1998	Three-time Lady Byng Trophy winner
Jaromir Jagr	RW	1990–2001	Five-time NHL scoring champion and nine-time All-Star
Mario Lemieux	C	1984–1997, 2000–2006	Three-time Hart Trophy winner; averaged 1.88 points per game
Evgeni Malkin	C	2006–present	Won the Conn Smythe Trophy after the 2009 finals

By the Numbers

TOP GOAL SCORER	**Mario Lemieux** 1984–1997, 2000–2006 690 goals	**TOP GOALTENDER**	**Tom Barrasso** 1988–2000 226 wins
TOP ASSISTS MAN	**Mario Lemieux** 1,033 assists	**TOP DEFENSEMAN**	**Paul Coffey** 1987–1992 440 points

Player & Owner

Mario Lemieux was so good that something special happened when he retired in 1997. The Hockey Hall of Fame waived its three-year waiting period and inducted him immediately. Lemieux purchased the Penguins in 1999. A year later he stunned the league by lacing up his skates again and becoming the first player/owner in league history.

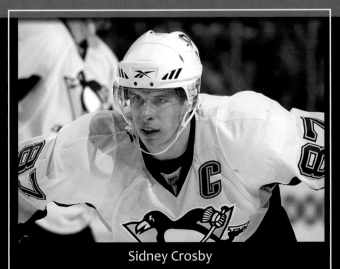
Sidney Crosby

Sid the Kid

Expectations were high for Sidney Crosby when he came into the NHL in 2005, but he's more than exceeded them. Crosby became the youngest team captain, the youngest scoring champion, and the youngest player to reach 200 points in league history.

53

SAN JOSE SHARKS

First Season: 1991–1992

Franchise Record: 630–618–121–75
Home Rink: HP Pavilion
(17,483 capacity) in San Jose, California

STANLEY CUPS
None

When the NHL expanded in 1967, California's San Francisco Bay Area got a team. But the Oakland Seals (later, the California Golden Seals) lasted just nine years before moving to Ohio and eventually folding. The league tried the West Coast again in the early 1990s. This time the San Jose Sharks stuck.

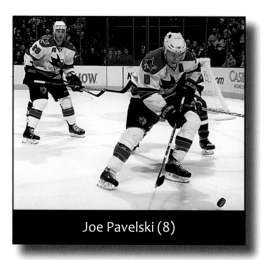
Joe Pavelski (8)

Legends & Stars

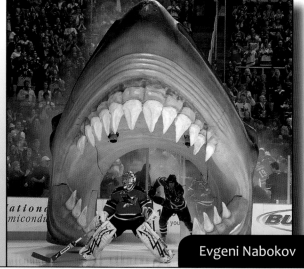
Evgeni Nabokov

Patrick Marleau	C	1997–present	San Jose made him the second overall draft pick in 1997
Evgeni Nabokov	G	1999–present	Calder Trophy winner in 2001
Owen Nolan	RW	1995–2003	Five-time All-Star Game selection
Joe Thornton	C	2005–present	NHL's leading scorer and Hart Trophy winner in 2006

By the Numbers

TOP GOAL SCORER	**Patrick Marleau** 1997–present 320 goals	**TOP GOALTENDER**	**Evgeni Nabokov** 1999–present 293 wins
TOP ASSISTS MAN	**Patrick Marleau** 373 assists	**TOP DEFENSEMAN**	**Mike Rathje** 1993–2004 128 assists

Third Year's a Charm

The Sharks won just 11 games in their second season, but they made a great leap forward in their third year. In 1993–1994 they went from 24 points in the standings to 82. They ended up going 33–35–16 and made the playoffs. But they weren't done there. In the first round, San Jose upset the top-seeded Red Wings in seven games. In the next series, however, the Sharks lost to the Toronto Maple Leafs in seven games.

Big Trade

Early in the 2005–2006 season, the Sharks pulled off a surprising trade when they got center Joe Thornton from the Boston Bruins. Thornton had been the No. 1 overall draft pick in 1997. He had his best season in his first year at San Jose. He led the NHL in scoring and won the Hart Trophy as MVP. With Thornton, the Sharks became one of the top teams, earning the league's best record in 2008–2009.

Joe Thornton (19)

ST. LOUIS BLUES

First Season: 1967–1968

Franchise Record: 1,457–1,374–432–79

Home Rink: Savvis Center
(19,260 capacity) in St. Louis, Missouri

STANLEY CUPS
None

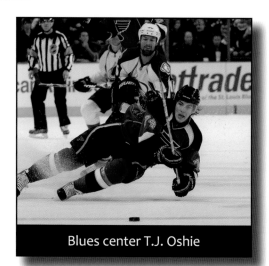
Blues center T.J. Oshie

The St. Louis Blues came into the NHL in the late 1960s when the league doubled in size. They immediately went to three Stanley Cup finals. Much of the success came from the aging but future Hall-of-Fame goalies Glenn Hall and Jacques Plante. The Blues remained regular playoff contenders, thanks to stars Brett Hull, Brian Sutter, and Chris Pronger.

Legends & Stars

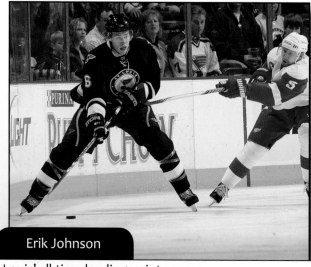
Erik Johnson

Bernie Federko	C	1976–1989	St. Louis' all-time leading point scorer
Brett Hull	RW	1988–1998	Hart Trophy winner in 1991
Erik Johnson	D	2007–present	No. 1 overall draft pick in 2006
Al MacInnis	D	1994–2004	Won the Norris Trophy in 1999
Chris Pronger	D	1995–2004	First defenseman to win the Hart Trophy since Bobby Orr
Brian Sutter	LW	1976–1988	Three-time All-Star played 12 seasons with the Blues

By the Numbers

TOP GOAL SCORER
Brett Hull
1988–1998
527 goals

TOP GOALTENDER
Mike Liut
1979–1985
151 wins

TOP ASSISTS MAN
Bernie Federko
1976–1989
721 assists

TOP DEFENSEMAN
Al MacInnis
1994–2004
452 points

Comeback Kids

Two of the best games in Blues history were come-from-behind, 6-5 overtime wins. In 1986 St. Louis pulled off "The Monday Night Miracle," erasing a 5-2 third-period deficit to force a Game 7 in the conference semifinals. In a 2000 regular-season game, the Blues were down 5-0 in the third period and came back to beat the Maple Leafs.

A Stop for "The Great One"

Wayne Gretzky is known as the greatest hockey player of all time. He made his career with the Oilers and the Kings. But he also had a short stint with the Blues, finishing the 1995–1996 season in St. Louis. Gretzky scored 21 points in 18 regular-season games and 16 points in 13 playoff games. But the next season, "The Great One" signed with the New York Rangers and finished his career there.

Wayne Gretzky scores his first goal after being traded to the St. Louis Blues.

TAMPA BAY LIGHTNING

Franchise Record: 504–671–112–77
Home Rink: St. Pete Times Forum
(19,758 capacity) in Tampa, Florida

STANLEY CUP
2004

First Season: 1992–1993

In 1992 the NHL added two new teams. It put one in the heart of hockey country, Ottawa, which had a team in the league until the 1930s. It put the other along the Gulf Coast of Florida and called it the Tampa Bay Lightning. But the Lightning hasn't played like an outsider. The team has been to the playoffs five times and became the southern-most team in the league to win a championship.

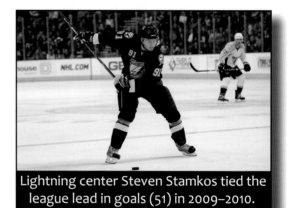
Lightning center Steven Stamkos tied the league lead in goals (51) in 2009–2010.

Legends & Stars

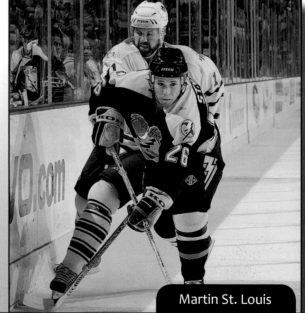
Martin St. Louis

Vincent Lecavalier	C	1998–present	Four-time All-Star led NHL in goals in 2007
Brad Richards	C	2000–2008	Won Conn Smythe and Lady Byng trophies in 2004
Martin St. Louis	RW	2000–present	Led NHL in scoring and was Hart Trophy winner in 2004

By the Numbers

TOP GOAL SCORER	**Vincent Lecavalier** 1998–present 326 goals	**TOP GOALTENDER**	**Nikolai Khabibulin** 2000–2004 83 wins
TOP ASSISTS MAN	**Vincent Lecavalier** 413 assists	**TOP DEFENSEMAN**	**Dan Boyle** 2002–2008 253 points

Magical Season

The Lightning had many heroes on their way to winning the Stanley Cup in 2004. Goalie Nikolai Khabibulin had five shutouts and Brad Richards scored 12 goals in the playoffs. League MVP Martin St. Louis scored a double-overtime goal in Game 6 of the finals. Ruslan Fedotenko scored both Tampa Bay goals in the Game 7 clincher.

2004 Stanley Cup champions

Famous First

In 1992 the Lightning made history when they signed goaltender Manon Rheaume. She was the first and only woman to play in the NHL. However, her only appearance came during an exhibition game.

TORONTO MAPLE LEAFS

First Season: 1917–1918

Franchise Record: 2,599–2,499–783–75
Home Rink: Air Canada Centre
(18,800 capacity) in Toronto, Ontario, Canada

STANLEY CUPS
1918, 1922, 1932, 1942, 1945, 1947, 1948, 1949, 1951, 1962, 1963, 1964, 1967

Toronto's NHL team was first known as the Arenas. They won a Stanley Cup under that nickname and another as the St. Pats before the legendary Conn Smythe took over the team in the 1920s. He changed the name to the Maple Leafs, after Canada's Maple Leaf Regiment that fought in World War I. Toronto captured 11 titles after the name change. The team has not reached the finals since winning the Cup in 1967.

Maple Leafs center Nik Antropov (11) played more than eight seasons with Toronto.

Legends & Stars

Tomas Kaberle

Syl Apps	C	1936–1943, 1945–1948	Led Toronto to three titles in the 1940s
Turk Broda	G	1936–1952	Two-time Vezina Trophy winner and five-time Cup winner
King Clancy	D	1930–1937	Longtime Senator led the Leafs to the 1932 title
Hap Day		1940–1950	Toronto coach led the Leafs to five championships
Tim Horton	D	1949–1970	Seven-time All-Star Game participant
Punch Imlach		1958–1969, 1979–1980	Leafs' coach won four Cups, including a "three-peat" in the 1960s
Tomas Kaberle	D	1998–present	Selected to the All-Star game four times
Ted Kennedy	C	1942–1955, 1956–1957	Won the Hart Trophy in 1955
Dave Keon	C	1960–1975	Eight-time All-Star won the Conn Smythe Trophy in 1967
Frank Mahovlich	LW	1956–1968	"The Big M" led the Leafs to four Stanley Cup wins

By the Numbers

TOP GOAL SCORER	**Mats Sundin** 1994–2008 420 goals	**TOP GOALTENDER**	**Turk Broda** 1936–1952 302 wins
TOP ASSISTS MAN	**Borje Salming** 1973–1989 620 assists	**TOP DEFENSEMAN**	**Tim Horton** 1949–1970 1,185 games played

More Hall of Famers

Of the more than 350 people inducted in the Hockey Hall of Fame, 55 have been part of the Maple Leafs organization. That's more than any other team in the NHL. Fittingly, the Hall is located in Toronto—Canada's largest city.

HOCKEY HALL OF FAME

Playing Hurt

Bob Baun might not be one of the Maple Leafs' greatest players, but he sure is a legend. In Game 6 of the 1964 Stanley Cup finals, a puck was shot and hit Baun, breaking his foot. He was taken off the ice on a stretcher, but he returned for overtime. With his foot numbed and taped, Baun scored the game-winning goal. Two nights later Toronto won Game 7 and their third-straight Stanley Cup.

VANCOUVER CANUCKS

First Season: 1970–1971

Franchise Record: 1,248–1,413–391–64
Home Rink: GM Place
(18,630 capacity) in Vancouver,
British Columbia, Canada

STANLEY CUPS
None

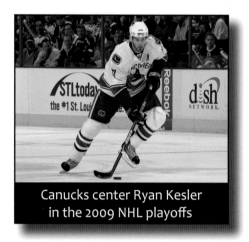

Canucks center Ryan Kesler
in the 2009 NHL playoffs

It took many years for the NHL to arrive in Vancouver, British Columbia. However, Canada's third-largest city had a long history with professional hockey before 1970. In 1915 a team called the Vancouver Millionaires played in the Pacific Coast Hockey Association. The Millionaires even won the Stanley Cup. As for the Canucks, they are still waiting to win their first championship.

Legends & Stars

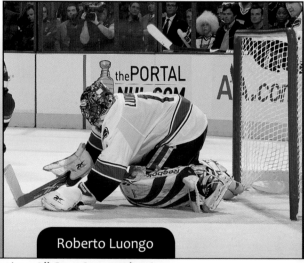

Roberto Luongo

Trevor Linden	RW	1988–1998, 2001–2008	Two-time All-Star Game selection
Roberto Luongo	G	2006–present	Played in three All-Star Games
Markus Naslund	LW	1996–2008	Won the Lester B. Pearson Award in 2003
Stan Smyl	RW	1978–1991	Was the Canucks' leading scorer upon retiring after 13 seasons

By the Numbers

TOP GOAL SCORER	**Markus Naslund** 1996–2008 346 goals
TOP GOALTENDER	**Kirk McLean** 1987–1998 211 wins
TOP ASSISTS MAN	**Henrik Sedin** 2000–present 434 assists
TOP DEFENSEMAN	**Dennis Kearns** 1971–1981 290 assists

Working Overtime

During the Canucks' run to the 1994 Stanley Cup finals, they won seven overtime games. In the first round Vancouver trailed the Flames three games to one before winning three-straight overtime games. Star forward Pavel Bure scored the double-overtime goal in Game 7 to send the Canucks to the championship series.

Twin Engines

In 1999 the Canucks made a trade to secure the second- and third-overall selections in the NHL draft. They used those picks to draft twin brothers Daniel and Henrik Sedin. The two have played on the same line together ever since. The twins have nearly identical numbers, with more than 460 points apiece. In 2009 they each signed a new contract to stay with Vancouver—and stay together.

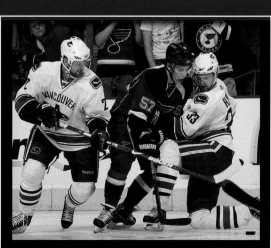

Daniel Sedin (22) and Henrik Sedin (33)

WASHINGTON CAPITALS

Franchise Record: 1,215–1,214–303–72

Home Rink: Verizon Center
(18,277 capacity) in Washington, D.C.

STANLEY CUPS
None

First Season: 1974–1975

With such players as Alex Ovechkin and Nicklas Backstrom, the Washington Capitals are one of the most exciting teams in the NHL. It wasn't always that way though. They won just eight games in their first season. At one point they lost 17 games in a row. But since cracking the playoffs in the early 1980s, they've seldom been left out of the postseason.

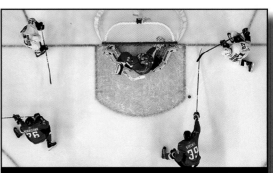

Capitals goalie Semyon Varlamov defends the net during the 2009 playoffs.

Legends & Stars

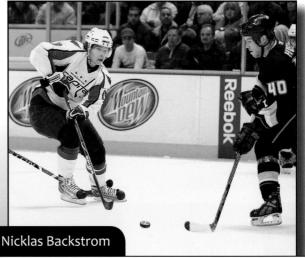

Nicklas Backstrom

Nicklas Backstrom	C	2007–present	2008 All-Rookie selection
Peter Bondra	RW	1990–2004	Five-time All-Star Game pick
Mike Gartner	RW	1979–1989	Seven-time All-Star Game selection
Dale Hunter	C	1987–1999	Ranks second all-time in penalty minutes
Rod Langway	D	1982–1993	Six-time All-Star Game pick and two-time Norris Trophy winner
Alex Ovechkin	LW	2005–present	Won a Calder and two Hart trophies

By the Numbers

TOP GOAL SCORER	**Peter Bondra** 1990–2004 472 goals	**TOP GOALTENDER**	**Olaf Kolzig** 1989–2008 301 wins
TOP ASSISTS MAN	**Michal Pivonka** 1986–1999 418 assists	**TOP DEFENSEMAN**	**Calle Johansson** 1989–2003 474 points

Alexander the Great

During his Calder Trophy-winning season, Alex Ovechkin scored what Capitals fans refer to as simply "the goal." Falling on the ice with his back to the goal and his hands above his head, the superstar still found a way to shoot the puck and put it in the net. Two years later, in 2008, Ovechkin became the first player to win the Hart, Ross, Pearson, and Richard trophies all in the same season.

Ironman Streak

Doug Jarvis started his career with the Montreal Canadiens in 1975 and ended it with the Hartford Whalers in 1987. In between he spent four seasons with the Capitals. Along the way, Jarvis never missed a game and set the NHL's consecutive-game streak of 964.

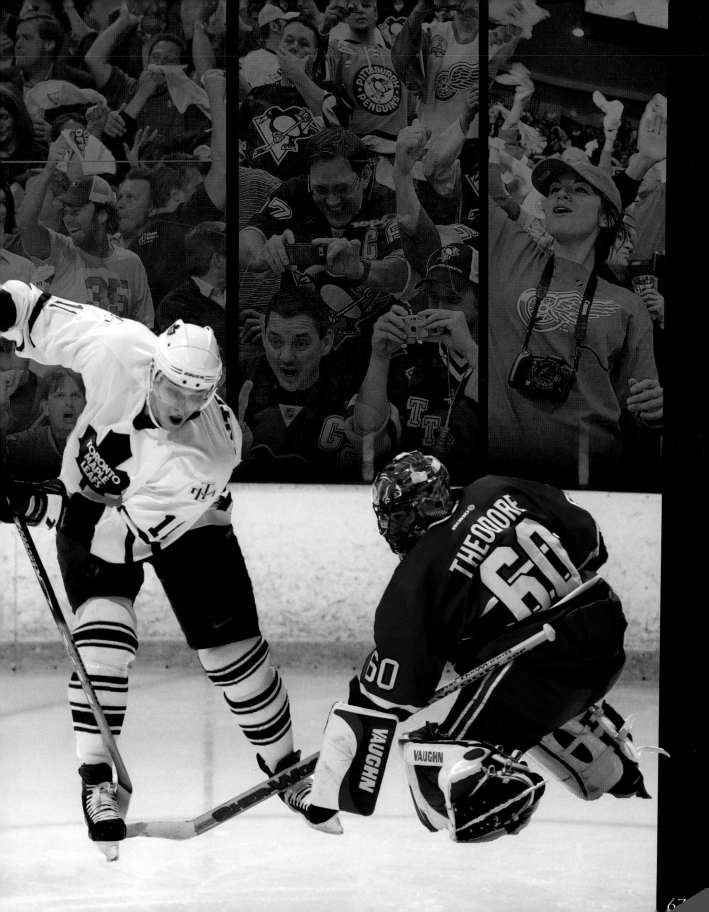

Edmonton Oilers

Calgary Flames

Vancouver Canucks

San Jose Sharks

Colorado Avalanche

Los Angeles Kings

Anaheim Ducks

Phoenix Coyotes

TEAM MAP

Montreal
Canadiens

Ottawa Senators

Boston
Bruins

Minnesota Wild

Toronto
Maple Leafs

Buffalo Sabres

New York Rangers

New York Islanders

Detroit
Red Wings

New Jersey Devils

Pittsburgh
Penguins

Philadelphia
Flyers

Chicago Blackhawks

Columbus
Blue Jackets

Washington
Capitals

St. Louis Blues

Carolina Hurricanes

Nashville Predators

Atlanta Thrashers

Dallas Stars

Tampa Bay Lightning

Florida Panthers

GLOSSARY

assist—a pass or a touch of the puck that sets up another player's goal
captain—the team leader; wears the letter C on his jersey
line—a group of three forwards—a center, a right wing, and a left wing
points—total scoring; goals plus assists

HOCKEY POSITIONS

center (C)—a forward who plays in the middle of the rink
defenseman (D)—one of two players who stays by the ice's blue line to help defend his goal
goaltender (G)—player who plays in front of the net and tries to stop the other team from scoring
left wing (LW)—forward who plays on the left side of the rink
right wing (RW)—forward who plays on the right side of the rink

NHL AWARD TROPHIES

Art Ross Trophy—leading point scorer
Bill Masterton Memorial Trophy—player who displays perseverance and dedication to hockey
Calder Memorial Trophy—rookie of the year
Conn Smythe Trophy—most valuable player of the playoffs
Frank J. Selke Trophy—top defensive forward
Hart Memorial Trophy—most valuable player
Jack Adams Award—coach of the year
James Norris Memorial Trophy—top defenseman
King Clancy Memorial Trophy—player who displays leadership on the ice and in the community
Lady Byng Memorial Trophy—player who displays gentlemanly conduct
Lester B. Pearson Award—MVP as voted on by the players
Maurice "Rocket" Richard Trophy—leading goal scorer
Vezina Trophy—top goaltender
William M. Jennings Trophy—goaltender with the lowest goals-against average

READ MORE

Goldner, John. *Hockey Talk: The Language of Hockey from A–Z.* Markham, Ontario: Fitzhenry & Whiteside, 2010.

Sandler, Michael. *Hockey: Miracle on Ice.* Upsets & Comebacks. New York: Bearport Publishing Company, 2006.

Shea, Therese. *Hockey Stars.* New York: Children's Press, 2007.

Thomas, Keltie. *Inside Hockey!: The Legends, Facts, and Feats that Made the Game.* Toronto: Maple Tree Press, 2008.

INTERNET SITES

FactHound offers a safe, fun way to find Internet sites related to this book. All of the sites on FactHound have been researched by our staff.

Here's all you do:

Visit *www.facthound.com*

Type in this code: 9781429648226

INDEX